What is the Dark Web?

The truth about the hidden part of the internet

Legal & Disclaimer

The information contained in this book and its contents is not designed to replace or take the place of any form of medical or professional advice; and is not meant to replace the need for independent medical, financial, legal or other professional advice or services, as may be required. The content and information in this book have been provided for educational and entertainment purposes only.

All content and information that can be found in the following book have been compiled from various sources that are deemed reliable and accurate to the Author's knowledge. The Author cannot guarantee the accuracy and validity and under no shape or form can or should be held liable for any errors and/or omissions found in this book. Further, changes are periodically made to this book as and when needed. Where appropriate and/or necessary, you must consult a professional (including but not limited to your doctor, attorney, financial advisor or such other professional advisor) before using any of the suggested remedies, techniques, or information in this book.

All attempts have been made to verify the information that is provided in this book. Neither the author nor the publisher assumes any responsibility for contrary interpretations of the subject matter herein. The author expressly disclaims all and any liability and responsibility to any person, whether a reader of this training manual or not, in respect of claims, losses or damage or any other matter, either direct or consequential arising out of or in relation to the use and reliance, whether

Contents

Introduction

You may have heard of the Dark Web and all the bad and shady things about it. It would almost seem that the Dark Web is a crook's haven. You can find various illegal products and services there. Nothing is off limits from drugs to guns and not to mention other unspeakable horrors that lurk within. Therefore, it would seem obvious that it should be destroyed and buried since nothing good could ever come out of it. However, some might say, that despite all of this, the Dark Web could offer a solution for one of modern society's biggest problems, privacy. Before we begin, I want to mention that this is a very difficult and complex subject. The information in this book is only meant to help you form your own opinion. So please try to maintain an open mind while dealing with this highly controversial information. That being said, let us begin.

The Dark Web is infamous for how people can remain anonymous while browsing, thus giving them the freedom to do everything they want. Of course, when you combine that with societies current structure, it inevitably leads to highly illegal activities. Drug dealing is one of them. Anonymity, in this case, can be achieved by using the Tor browser (more on that later), and it is one of the keys to the Dark Web. Many people mistake the Deep Web from the Dark Web and the two are often used interchangeably and incorrectly. So, how are they different?

There are three levels of the World Wide Web. The Surface Web, which is where most of us "surf". This level has everything discoverable by any main search engine of your internet browsers. The things you can find include various household products, news, and other information from today's social media. Pictures of our meals or funny cat videos have some of us hypnotized and almost blinded about the real world. The Surface Web is also under constant surveillance from the government. While the Dark Web seems to be infinitely vast to many people, it is merely a fraction of the entire internet (roughly 4 to 5 percent of the entire World Wide Web content).

The Deep Web represents all the websites that are not found by ordinary search engines. The Deep Web consists of all the data behind firewalls. Databases, business intranets, web archives, password-protected websites fall into the same category. The Deep Web is accessible but requires something like a password encrypted browser or a set of log-in details. The Deep Web is about 500 times larger than the Surface Web.

The Dark Web, however, can only be accessed by using certain browsers such as the Tor browser and it exists within the Deep Web. The content inside the Dark Web is purposely concealed. The URL is not as simple and understandable as "www.(websitename).com". It is more of a string of numbers and alphabets that ends in ".onion"

So, how does the Dark Web come into being? How is it bad? Is there any potential upside to the Dark Web? Before we delve deep into the history of the Dark Web, we must first understand the importance of privacy because anonymity is key in this story.

Why Is Privacy So Important?

The Dark Web promises anonymity, and that is why it has millions of users worldwide. Maybe it does not seem as important to you because you have nothing to hide. However, following the incident with Edward Snowden and the NSA, as well as the more recent Facebook privacy controversy known as the Cambridge Analytics controversy, it became clear that privacy and anonymity are very important to many people. In fact, there is a photo of Facebook CEO Mark Zuckerberg who had a tape over the webcam on his laptop, which suggests that he too is concerned about his privacy and so should you.

In the middle 1800s, you didn't need much to have some privacy. Just some locked doors, windows, and you were shielded from the outside world. Privacy was a gift that many people took for granted. With the advancement of technology in the form of computers and the internet, it has become almost impossible to shield yourself from the outside world. Especially not with some closed doors and windows because the electronic device you are using right now to read this book is the window to the outside world. Even if you sit at home alone in your room, you are not really as private as you think. Your online activities are being monitored. This, however, begs the question, is it a good thing or a bad one? Even if you don't have anything to hide, there are still many other reasons why you should be concerned about your privacy.

For one, it limits the government's power and that of private companies. If they know so much about every one of us, they can easily influence us in ways we could never imagine. Take private companies for example. If they know what food you like, then you can expect to see advertisements for it whenever you browse the internet. They want you to buy their products, and the only way to do it is by offering convincing advertisements. In addition, your personal data could actually be sold to those companies. However, your personal data should not be treated as mere goods. More so one could argue that you should be compensated if your personal data is sold. Still, you don't get a penny from it. The same could be said for governments. Politics is more of a popularity contest nowadays. Politicians need to know what makes the citizens happy, so they can promise all of those things when, in reality, they know some of them could be never be really delivered.

Privacy is also about respecting each individual. Many people just want some privacy and they should have it. It is outright insulting if anyone ignores that. Of course, there are important things that outweigh a person's privacy, but it should count among one of the last resorts to solve a problem. In Edward Snowden's words, he compared this situation to a person holding a gun to your head and saying, "Don't worry. I won't shoot. Trust me." Although the US government meant well when they wanted to have the ability to see into its citizens' devices in order to stop terrorist attacks, the message they're sending is different. This invasion of privacy simply shows a lack of respect for the individual, and it is like saying that you care about your own interests but not the civilians'.

Privacy also allows people to manage their own reputations. How we are seen and judged affect our friendships, opportunities, and well-being. Even if we cannot fully control how others see us, at least privacy gives us a chance to protect our own reputation against both falsehoods but also certain truths. People are misjudged because they are misunderstood. However, knowing more about a person does not mean a more accurate judgment. In fact, many people judge very quickly and falsely. One great example of this was a TED presentation conducted by Jon Ronson. In it, he stated how simple it is for a tweet to ruin a person's life. He talked about Justine Sacco and how her tweet which was originally meant to be a joke caused an uproar that eventually ruined her life. What happened had, of course, nothing to do with privacy, but it showed how quickly people judge and jump to conclusions. They judge hastily, with hypocrisy, and often out of context. The only way to be protected in these situations is in the form of privacy.

On a more intimate level, privacy is a sanctuary we could retreat to. All of us have social boundaries, both physical and informational. All of us just want to have a place to be alone and have some "alone" time. Having these boundaries allow us to determine how close you want other people to be. You draw the line, and everyone should respect it. Without these boundaries, there will always be awkward social situations and every person has a certain way of dealing with them. Some can get over it pretty quickly others recur to alcohol, drugs, overeating and even violence to cope with social traumas. You want people to know about you, but to get the chance to see the real you.

Trust goes hand in hand with privacy. In any relationship, be it social or professional, one can never stress the importance of trust enough. If you do not respect a person's privacy, then you don't trust them. Some parents read their children's diary to make sure that they are doing alright. However, some children see it as a violation of trust. The same could be said for a government and its people. By violating a person's privacy, their freedoms of thought, speech, social and political activities become also violated. All of us behave differently when we are being watched. In other words, we are not truly ourselves when we know that someone is watching us. Even animals behave differently when there are people watching.

In the most extreme scenarios, the government could attempt to control the citizen's thoughts. By controlling the media output and the information flow for every individual. And let's be honest, such a case is all too familiar to most of us. It is a dystopian future that we all do not want to have. Without privacy, all of us would lose our individuality. When our speech and thoughts are monitored, we would become something akin to robots. All of us would just conform to certain standards set by the government. If they can monitor our thoughts, then they could just as easily brainwash everyone. Such a future keeps some people awake at night. Sadly, we are already well on our way there, starting with the loss of net neutrality which puts an end to a free, open internet where all contents are treated equally. Certain companies can now control what you see on the internet, and if we do not do something soon, then things are only going to get worse.

Privacy is such an important thing for many people. Unfortunately, it is currently being threatened. Something must be done because one privacy violation could lead to many more along the way. It must be protected. Our online privacy is at risk, but is there a place where we could all retreat to? A place where everyone can be truly anonymous? Does this sanctuary exist? Luckily, there is a technology that could protect our online privacy. It led to the birth of what is known as the Dark Web, and it has been with us for a few decades already.

What is the Dark Web?

With the internet's continuous growth in the mid-1990s, the society is transformed on a global scale. Among those changes, the biggest one is the rise of instant communication.

If you have an internet connection, you could talk to pretty much everyone else across the globe as long as they are also connected. By 2000, there were over 350 million users. Since then, another concern arose with the growth of the internet. The internet was not designed to keep the users anonymous. In fact, everything that you say and do on the internet can be recorded and tracked back to you.

While this seems like a sensible feature since the police and other authorities could trace online evidence back to the perpetrator. However, some were concerned about their privacy. In the mid-1990s, the United States federal government was one of them.

A group of mathematicians and computer scientists working for the United States Navy known as the Naval Research Laboratory (NRL) started the development of a new technology that would allow for anonymous bi-directional communication where the destination and the source could not be determined by a mid-point.

Basically, the people working for the US government created a system that allows anonymous communication over the internet. However, they quickly realized that in order to achieve anonymity, the technology would have to be released to the public. It makes no sense to wear a mask to conceal your identity when everyone else cannot wear it. Everyone will know that it is you. The same concept applies to this technology. If the US agents are authorized to use this technology whereas nobody else can, then whenever an anonymous connection came through, everyone could tell that the CIA was looking at their website, which defeats the purpose of anonymity.

Therefore, the NRL released their onion routing technology which was known as Tor under an open source license. TOR stands for The Onion Router and you need it in order to access the network of onion routers. Nowadays, there are millions of people around the world using the Tor browser.

Here, it is worth noting that the Tor browser can also be used for your mundane, daily browsing. Tor allows the users to browse anonymously, which is one of the reasons why so many people have been using it. You can check your email, message your friends, watch funny cat videos, and do other things using this browser. However, the Tor browser also has a hidden service. It allows you to access the Dark Web.

It is because of this animosity that makes the Dark Web a perfect ground for criminals to conduct their dirty business. In October 2013, the FBI took down an online drug marketplace known as the Silk Road that had been operating for about 2 years. It was then that the public began to realize that the Dark Web exists. The FBI arrested the administrator but that had little impact on the drug trade in the Dark Web. In fact, more websites offering the same services continue to pop up and are inevitably but slowly taken down. It is not just the drug business that exists on in the Dark Web. There are a lot of other illegal businesses operating there as well.

Another example of a service available on the Dark Web is the assassination services. However, assassinations are unlikely to have occurred. The problem is a lack of evidence since anyone can set up a Darknet website and claim to do anything for any reason, especially if money is involved. One such website was hacked, and it turned out that it was merely a scam to trick criminals out of their money, or at least that was what the admins said in their leaked messages. Still, it is impossible to tell if they were telling the truth or not.

A study from 2016 found that about 1,500 out of 2,700 active .onion websites on the Tor network contain illicit content, which is well over half. However, only 3 to 6 percent of all the Tor users actually use these hidden services. In other words, only 3-6% use the Dark Web. A majority only use them to protect their privacy and browse the Surface Web anonymously. They have never visited a .onion website. That would suggest that all the horrors going on inside the Dark Web may not be as vast as you think. However, horrors they still are. So, why is it so difficult to track and take down an illicit Dark Web site?

Taking Down the Elusive Illicit Websites

Shutting down illegal Dark Web sites is a lot harder than it may seem. Government agents would take them all down if it were as easy as taking down a website on the Surface Web. Even Pirate Bay, a notorious file-sharing website, has proven itself to be a challenge, and it was a website right on the Surface Web. Taking down a Dark Web site is a challenge on a different level.

Running an illegal market in the Dark Web has a lot of risks involved, so everyone did everything in their power to remain anonymous. Therefore, people who are running the markets are well-hidden behind some of the best privacy protection software. With multiple layers of protection in place, taking them all down to find the true culprit would take a lot of time and money. The notorious drug marketplace Silk Road had been operating for 2 years before it was taken down. Just a few months later, Silk Road 2.0 was launched and taken down the next year. Silk Road 3.0 was launched a few hours after that. Basically, it is faster and cheaper for a criminal to launch an illegal website than it is for authorities to take one down. To make matters worse, we are talking about only one illegal business in the Dark Web. There are a lot more down there offering different illicit services. Taking all of them down would be nearly impossible.

If only anonymity were not there, then the authorities would be able to find the culprit easier. Alas, many people want to have just that. There is no way to limit the onion routing technology to only the innocent civilians and government agents. It is worth noting again that this onion routing technology was intended for the government agents' uses only. However, it was proven that limiting its use will only render this technology useless. When they released it to the public, criminals took the opportunity to expand their business online.

So, why not take everything down? If you cannot track and shut down all of the illegal Dark Web websites, wouldn't it be wise to "bite the bullet" and shut the Dark Web completely? Even if some of the licit websites will be affected, at least it will put an end to the criminal activities online, right? According to a survey conducted by a Canadian think tank of over 24,000 people, approximately %71 of them believed that the Dark Web should be shut down entirely. Many people probably imagine that the Dark Web is a singular place where all the criminals conduct their dirty business and that all it takes is an FBI raid. Sadly, it does not work that way.

Shutting down the Dark Web is impossible. Doing so would mean shutting down every single site and relay. For example, if we are to shut Tor down, then we would need to shut down more than 7,000 secret nodes worldwide at the same time. We mentioned before how challenging it was to shut down Pirate Bay. Imagine how hard it is to shut down a network of sites that have encrypted communication and hidden IP addresses that are hosted worldwide.

To make matters worse, there are many networks out there that offer the key to the Dark Web. Tor alone has 7,000 secret nodes worldwide. There are other networks as well such as I2P or Freenet. All of these networks function similarly to Tor and shutting all of them down means an astronomical number of nodes needed to be taken down at the same time worldwide. An operation of that scale requires a lot of resources and time, which would make the entire thing impossible. There is nothing we could really do about it. So, it's pretty safe to say that the Dark Web and all of its contents are here to stay.

The Onion Router

Before we can understand whether Tor is actually secured, we need to understand how the technology works. We mentioned earlier about anonymous bi-directional communication in which the source or the destination cannot be determined by a midpoint. This is accomplished by creating an overlay network. This network is built on top of another network, which in this case is the internet. Simply put, your traffic goes through the overlay network instead of the normal, unencrypted internet. There are many types of overlay networks, but a network would be classified as a Darknet if it uses the onion routing technology.

A Darknet can only be accessed by specific software or authorization. Again, there was a misunderstanding between the Darknet and the Dark Web. In simpler terms, the Darknet is the road which you take to access the websites which are the Dark Web.

Let us take the Tor network for instance. It runs through the computer servers of thousands of volunteers across the globe. Your information, or data, is bundled into a packet that is encrypted as it enters the network. Then, Tor takes away the part of the packet's header, which has the information about the sender. After that, Tor encrypts the rest of the addressing information known as the packet wrapper. The modified and encrypted data packet is finally routed through many servers (or relays) on the way to the destination. The way Tor encrypts, routes, and reroutes your data packet is similar to how a person is trying to shake a pursuer off by taking a roundabout path.

It is impossible to know what the encrypted data contains even if you managed to intercept and decrypt the data packet at its relay. Each relay only contains information about where the data packet came from, and where it should go next, and it only rewraps the package before sending it on. That way, the data packet's path through the Tor network can never be fully traced.

While there are some forms of encryption protocols for the regular internet. Those protocols are not as secured as you may be led to believe. A skilled hacker or a determined government agent would find it relatively easy to intercept, decrypt, and learn about the information that you sent through the internet.

However, if the people working for the government designed Tor, then is it truly safe? Well, as an online anonymizer, Tor was actually designed to be very secure for its users.

According to the documents that were leaked by Edward Snowden, the NSA had actually tried to infiltrate, crack, or weaken any encryption that the agency does not control. This comes as really bad news, as it proves that the US government is actively trying to spy on its own people. According to an interview with Edward Snowden conducted by John Oliver, he explained in detail how the US government managed to snatch most (if not all) of the details that go in, out, or circulate within the country. It has become clear that all independent encryption and online communication services have become a suspect, and Tor is no exception.

This online anonymity network is, therefore, a high-priority target for the NSA, according to Bruce Schneier, who is a cryptography expert helping the British newspaper The Guardian to analyze its archive of documents leaked by Snowden. Luckily, another document from him confirmed that the NSA cannot crack Tor, although it has developed a workaround.

This workaround is based on the vulnerability of the Firefox browser. The Tor browser is based on Firefox. So, it's no surprise that both share similar weakness which the NSA could exploit. Of course, this vulnerability has been patched in the recent updates, and so Tor user's anonymity remained protected.

The documents also tell another interesting fact. Because the NSA said that they could not crack Tor and that they attempted to work around it by using a browser exploit, it proves that Tor's protocol was tough enough that NSA could not break it. They could not even do traffic analysis on the Tor network.

However, Tor has come under security setbacks in the form of cyber attacks. This presents a problem for its users, and the need for an alternative anonymous browser arose. All of them are different networks and use different encryption solutions to protect their users.

Take I2P, for example. I2P offers anonymous communication as well. It that regard, it can be considered better than Tor because it is faster, more secured, and it has fully distributed and self-organizing capability. Tor allows for a bi-directional anonymous communication. I2P takes it a step further by making it unidirectional instead. That way the route gets even more confusing for those who attempt to hack and steal data.

Since Tor was becoming a prime suspect for the NSA, everyone tried to find alternative ways to get into the Dark Web without the government interfering. Of course, most of the users just wanted to remain anonymous when they browse online. A few others wanted, however, to remain so because they want to continue conducting illicit businesses.

Since the discovery of the Silk Road, mainstream media attempted to convince the public that the surface web is merely a thin layer sitting on top of an enormous criminal underground. That alone has some truth to it but let us not forget that there are also legitimate websites on the Dark Web, although fewer in number. In fact, some of them are launched for a good cause. Some are there for journalists, whereas others are support networks for survivors of abuse or other atrocities. The Dark Web is not as "dark" as you may have been led to believe. In fact, there is something we could all learn from and use it as a foundation to build something better for mankind.

In Defense of the Dark Web

From the creation of the Dark Web, many have seen how it easily became a haven for criminals. However, let us not forget what the Dark Web was intended to do. Its main purpose was to provide its users the anonymity that the Surface Web could not. A person's privacy goes hand in hand with their safety, and that is exactly why many people prefer using the Tor browser. The Dark Web is a censorship-free world, but also a hiding place for criminals, whistleblowers, and political activists alike.

Anonymity is the name of the game here. We mentioned before that the Dark Web is the host to many criminal businesses. But if everyone is anonymous, then how do they conduct business? The answer might surprise you. In a world of criminals, trust is very essential and the first thing you want to know before you buy anything is knowing who the seller is. After all, why would you trust someone with your money when you don't even know who he is? Especially when you buy something illegal, knowing the seller is very crucial. This trust problem goes both ways. What if the customer is actually an undercover cop? Mutual trust is important, but so is identity. Now, I am not trying to defend any illegal activity here. That whole part is of course extremely bad. However, some problems that arose in those markets gave birth to some interesting solutions and we could all benefit by analyzing and learning from them.

Jamie Bartlett once conducted a Ted Talk about the Dark Web. He ventured out to the Dark Web to experience it first-hand. What he discovered was something truly astounding.

In the harsh environment of the Dark Web, everyone needs to be innovative and clever in order to keep up with the industry. He went into one of the Dark Web's drug trade websites and realized that the layout of that website was very familiar with that of conventional online marketplaces. In his presentation, he showed the audience an image of the Silk Road website, which was a host to many drug trades. There were many illegal products. Interestingly enough, you could find out the details of the product as well as its price just like on any normal website. Funny enough, there was even a report button.

The method of payment was cryptocurrency, (which we will address later in the book) more specific Bitcoin. You would have to enter an address (which, for obvious reasons, could not be a home address) and the product will eventually arrive. Now, we mentioned before that everyone is anonymous and that conducting business can be a risky thing. However, it worked most of the time. Why is that?

The entire process worked because of the user reviews and how important they were. It is actually possible to know who a person is without knowing his identity. Even if you do not know who the seller is, you can still recognize him after an alias. That is crucial. The sellers have to build up their reputation under that name. Let us not forget that trust is very fragile in the Dark Web, and so the only way a buyer can trust a seller is by his reputation. That comes in the form of feedback from the previous customers.

Here is a quick scenario, suppose that you are looking to buy something illegal. On the Dark Web, you find a website that sells just that. When you go in there, you will see numerous products related to what you are looking for. You browse through all of them to find the product that you want. Before buying, you look at the seller's name. Let us assume that his alias is Mr. Evil. You look at his review and it is overwhelmingly positive. You know you can trust this person (although his real name is of course not Mr. Evil) and you order your product. You pay in Bitcoin, and you put in the address of where you want it to be delivered. After a while, the product arrives and you may give a review to Mr. Evil so others could see if he is trustworthy or not. Does this process sound familiar? Well of course it does, because it is the same process we follow when we order a book or furniture online. What causes this need for trustworthiness is plain simple. It's called competition.

Since there are many websites out there offering illegal services, competition can be pretty fierce. With competition comes the need for creativity and innovation. Prices go down, quality goes up, the sellers become friendly and treat you as a valuable customer. Why? They know that there is always another vendor out there willing to go the extra mile and be polite to you, so you would buy from him again.

When you look at it, the only difference is in the products that are being sold. If you take the drugs or other illegal services out of the way, what are you left with? The same competitive market that you see on the Surface Web. You will find exclusive deals, one-offs, free delivery and buy-one-get-one-free deals in there just as often as you would find similar deals on the Surface Web.

During his presentation, Jamie Barlett recounted his experience when he wanted to study the customer service offered by one of these online markets. He put himself in the position of a customer and chose a buyer. Jamie reviewed the terms and conditions and the refund policy. To his surprise, and everyone's surprise, everything looked very professional and the refund policy was very generous, not to mention that the delivery time was also quick. The buyer was very communicative and did anything to please the customer. This just helps to outline the point made earlier. To survive in a competitive market, one has to be innovative and adaptive.

After analyzing that email, one thing became obviously clear. The customer is always king. In the Dark Web, that is no exception. When vendors have such a consumer-centric attitude that can be a good but also a bad thing. For one, it makes drug distribution a lot more comfortable for consumers. For the vendors, there would be more competition as the result of how easily accessible drugs are. On the other hand, when you take the drugs out of the way, you see a consumer's paradise where the customer is king and where you can find cheap, high-quality goods and services. This could possibly be the future of the online marketplace.

Aside from the customer service, there is also another issue when it comes to operating a shop in the Dark Web. That is the payment system. If you pay by credit card, then the authorities could easily see the transaction and trace your purchase back to you, which defeats the purpose of remaining anonymous. Then there is a risk of being scammed, which we are all too familiar with. Even on the Surface Web, some people somewhere are always trying to pull something off, so they could get some easy money. Fortunately, they often get caught in the end because of how easy the authorities are able to find the identity of the culprit. But what if that identity is hidden? How does the payment system work in the Dark Web? How is it protected?

We mentioned earlier that everyone pays using Bitcoin. However, there was a flaw in the system. Some dealers were running away with people's Bitcoin before they would deliver the products. To put an end to this problem, the community came up with a solution known as multi-signature escrow payments.

Upon purchasing an item, the customer would send their Bitcoin to a neutral, secure third digital wallet. The vendor would see the deposit and be confident that they could send the product to the customer. The customer then could sign the transaction along with the vendor to confirm it. The money would then be transferred.

What if the vendor or the customer wants to cheat? That would be impossible since there are three players in this transaction. The vendor, the customer, and the administrator of the third-party website. The transaction needs two out of the three approvals before the money could be transferred. If the vendor attempts to cheat, then the customer could report it to the admin and the money would then be transferred back to the customer. Otherwise, if the customer tries to cheat and not pay for the product, the vendor could just contact the administrator and the money would be transferred to the vendor. This system is simple, elegant, and it works.

However, there was yet another flaw. Every Bitcoin transaction is recorded in a public ledger. There is no anonymity in that. It is not difficult for the authorities to track the transaction and trace it back to you. A way to obscure this transaction was needed. This problem gave birth to yet another brilliant solution. They came up with a tumbling service.

Basically, hundreds of people would send their Bitcoin into a single address where they were mixed up and then sent to the right recipients with the right amount in different Bitcoins. This process can be called a micro-laundering system, very similar to money laundering. That way, it became impossible to track down who made the purchase and from whom.

It would appear that the illegal market is slowly growing in the Dark Web, but it is worth noting that they are operating in a harsh environment. Even though the Surface Web is pretty much inhabitable for criminals, surviving in the Dark Web can be pretty challenging. The vendors are at risk of being discovered, arrested, and having their own website shut down by the authorities, and yet despite all of that, many managed to escape the grasp. In this book, I do not try to defend their actions. I just want to outline how operating in such an environment forced people to come up with some incredible solutions. Now the war against crime requires many sacrifices and the people who made those sacrifices deserve our deepest respect. The good part is that by learning from the innovations that were created in the Dark Web, we could improve our thinking, advance our methods and use them in the combat against crime.

It is also worth mentioning again that people are becoming increasingly concerned with their privacy. Several surveys consistently showed that people take their privacy very seriously. In fact, our worries are growing. There are many things we should be worried about when it comes to our online privacy. Ever since the revelations from Edward Snowden, many people are trying to find ways to protect their privacy. Millions of people use Tor on a daily basis, and a majority of them uses it for very legitimate reasons, or even for mundane tasks. There are hundreds of activists around the world working on ways to protect your online privacy such as default encrypted messaging services.

A good example is Ethereum, which is a project that tries to connect millions of computers across the globe and utilize their unused hard drives to establish a distributed internet. That way it becomes virtually impossible to block the flow of information or, in other words, to censor it. There are also other familiar projects such as MaidSafe or Twister.

The more of us join the Dark Web, the more content there will be, and it will become more and more enticing and interesting. The Dark Web is not a drug dealer's den anymore. In fact, Surface Web titans have started pushing licit content in forms of a Dark Web site and by setting an example, they could convince others to do the same thing.

Speaking of freedom of speech and democracy, the Dark Web could have other uses than just being an anonymous and infinitely vast marketplace. It could also serve as an important source of information for everyone who could not find it on the surface web. Websites for whistleblowers, political activists, or even survival support networks are not uncommon in the Dark Web. Many media outlets have told stories of how the Dark Web is a scary place where criminals thrive, but that is not the case anymore.

Certain journalists or blog writers, out of curiosity, decided to dive deep into the darkness in order to find out if the stories are true. They found gun dealers, drug merchants, and other illegal businesses, but they also found things that were purposely censored from the Surface Web for political reasons. Websites such as We Fight Censorship, Reporters without Borders, and many popular newspapers that offer anonymous file submission sites could be found in the darkness. There are also support networks like those for victims of human rights abuse and other social diseases. By considering these aspects, the good part of a Dark Web starts to become clear. However, where did it all go so wrong? Why do so few people know about this?

It seems that the Dark Web's reputation was ruined by the emergence and the subsequent discovery of the Silk Road back in 2011. Not only is it an underground digital marketplace that eventually became a drug dealing hotspot, but it is also one of the first to utilize cryptocurrency as a means of transferring money. Its value amounted up to $2.4 billion in 2013, according to Business Insider. The media was quick to jump to conclusions and wrote extensively about how the Dark Web was a place for criminals to conduct their business. However, Ross Ulbricht, who was the creator of Silk Road, argued that the website was originally intended for people to purchase and sell items without being interfered by the State which would impose taxes or delay the delivery. Now when you think about it, it was actually a very smart idea. Sadly, his explanations were censored from the rest of the world and only a few people understood his intentions.

In reality, it seems that the mainstream media has been scaremongering everyone into believing that the Dark Web is a forbidden zone. According to James Chappell, CTO and Co-Founder of Digital Shadows, a global company monitoring online risk across the open, Deep and Dark Web, he argued that 95% of the sites on Tor are harmless. Most people just read about the Dark Web and immediately assumed that its contents are all illegal. He went on to explain that the Dark Web serves as a sanctuary where everyone goes to for that privacy that they need. He believed that privacy is a human right, and it must not be violated. A core member of the Tor browser movement, Jacob Appelbaum, also supports his view. He argued that surveillance is a threat to the fundamental core of democracy and that he started using Tor because he knew that he was not free.

As the awareness of surveillance and the need to protect one's privacy grows, the Tor browser starts to gain more and more popularity. The team behind Tor stated that they wish to give its users the security and privacy back to them.

HackerOne, which is a company that offers ethical hacking services by attempting to hack into their clients' systems in order to expose their vulnerabilities, had Tor as one of their clients. The Global Communications Director of HackerOne, Lauren Koszarek, pointed out the movement of good deeds that have been carried out in the Dark Web. This community of hackers has donated over $100,000 to charities such as Doctors Without Borders, Freedom of Press Foundation, and even UNICEF. Lauren then discussed how people have misconceptions about the Dark Web. She stated that the name "Dark Web" brings the assumption that it is a vicious world when in reality it is merely the unknown. We tend to stay away from the unknown because it is scary. Just because we do not know what is really going on in the Dark Web, we assume that it is bad. To make matters worse, the mainstream media makes it scarier when they cover only the ugly side that can be found there. So, why is there such a need to downplay the Dark Web?

Experts or those who have been in the Dark Web argued that it is misunderstood. They argue that it can be a very powerful tool for democracy as it allows people to have a voice in a world full of censorship. Some other individuals dismissed the idea and labeled it as dangerous, twisted, and outright illegal. Is mainstream media alone responsible for propagating this idea?

A Dark Web Documentary Filmmaker, Alex Winter, argued that the mainstream media is not alone in this scaremongering effort. With a tool so powerful that it can lead information to bypass the government's censorship, you can guess that they are not the only ones interested in limiting this technology. Other companies and government agencies have been actively spreading false information about privacy tools in order to keep the people on the Surface Web where their online activities can be observed, and their personal data can be collected. Big data has become an extremely lucrative industry and the biggest online media titans alone made over $9 billion in the second quarter of 2017 and that only from user advertisement. They just collect our personal data and sell it to interested companies. That way these companies could produce advertisements that would entice potential customers to buy their products. Snowden has also proved just how invasive the US government's surveillance methods are.

Mainstream media, tech companies, and government agencies have been trying their best to label the Dark Web as the forbidden zone. They have been largely successful, but people are slowly becoming more aware of the lies and more worried about their own privacy in the comfort of their own home. The idea that the Dark Web is more of a sanctuary where people can be free from surveillance is slowly emerging. This was achieved with the help of the few who dared to venture in and face the unknown and then came back and shared it with the world.

The Dark Web has a lot of potentials. It can actually improve the future of the internet. The government would have no power there, and everyone would be free from surveillance. People who have lost their voice can find it in the Dark Web and there would be people listening to them. Without the government's influence over the citizens, they could finally have the freedom to express themselves. To top it all off, they could do it with impunity because their identity is hidden. If there are enough people in the Dark Web, the face of it could change. However, this is a dangerous road that must be taken slowly and with care. Done wrong, it could cause a lot of harm to the world. All we can do is learn from the good side and try to build on top of it.

To sum it all up, the Dark Web is not all bad, as we are led to believe. It is undeniable that there are criminal activities operating in the darkness, but the Surface Web is also a host to some illegal activities. While the bad side of the Dark Web cannot and should not be ignored, it is equally important that we get a sense of what the entire story looks like. Because the truth should be available to all of us.

The Dark Web and Cryptocurrencies

We mentioned how cryptocurrencies (most notably, Bitcoin) were used to carry out transactions. Just like any other physical currencies, cryptocurrencies would be worthless if no one would give value to them. Some argued that the value of Bitcoin would not be as high without the Dark Web. In the last few years, a correlation could be seen between the value of Bitcoin and the growing use of the Dark Web.

In order to fully comprehend how the Dark Web affects Bitcoin, we must understand how large the illicit e-commerce is. According to Coindesk, the combined daily volumes of six drug markets amount up to $650,000. Researchers said that the total is between $300,000 and $500,000 a day. These large sums are not going from the customer to the vendor in form of physical money. They go through as Bitcoin.

Meanwhile, there is a legitimate payment processor that converts Bitcoin purchases into fiat known as Bitpay. As the name suggests, Bitpay allows customers to purchase online goods and services with digital currency, which replaces credit cards. That gives everyone a means to make purchases with their Bitcoin, even criminals.

Even with the Silk Road taken down, cryptocurrencies still have a very strong tie with the Dark Web, and it drives the industry forward whereas no other currencies can. A digital black market needs a digital equivalent of cash, and Bitcoin and other cryptocurrencies fit perfectly into this role. There is no one really in charge of the network of cryptocurrency, so there is no one to block illegal transactions.

There is a flaw with cryptocurrency, however. Although identity verification is unnecessary, it does not mean that you are completely anonymous. After all, all transactions are publicly recorded in a public ledger. It is true that it is not possible to tell exactly who is buying an item using Bitcoins, but the authorities are able to identify the culprit based on the pattern of the transaction and then tie it to a real-world identity. This has already been proven when the authorities were able to show that the founder of Silk Road 2.0 had cashed out about $270,000 worth of Bitcoin and used some of that money to purchase a brand-new car. While it is not clear how the authorities did that, at least we know that transactions using cryptocurrencies do not give full anonymity to its user. Hiding Bitcoin earnings can be therefore very difficult. This gave birth to the idea, as we mentioned in previous chapters, to the micro laundering technique.

The concept of how micro laundering avoids detection is very simple. The authorities can track the source of the money to the recipient. All transactions using cryptocurrencies are recorded, and so they know how much was transferred. They do not know who the people behind the transactions were, but they know how much money was involved. All you need is a midpoint between where the money comes from and where it goes, and a lot of other transactions using the same midpoint. Here is an example:

Suppose that you are looking to buy a cheap sofa on the Dark Web. You found the perfect deal and you made the purchase. Your product arrives, and you confirm your payment. How is your money transferred? Your money will go to an address that offers tumbling services for a certain cryptocurrency. For your convenience, we will say that you send your money in Litecoin. But your money is not going in there alone. There are hundreds of sources that link the money up to the address as well as in other cryptocurrency forms. Then, everyone's money will be mixed up and then sent to the vendor in different forms of cryptocurrency. If you sent in Litecoin to the tumbling website, then what comes out is Zcash or some other coin. However, the amount is exactly the same, just in different cryptocurrency.

It is relatively easy for authorities to find out where your money goes if your transaction is the only one that is being registered. However, when there are hundreds of transactions going through, it can get very confusing. The authorities may know how much money is sent to the website for one transaction, but it is a mystery where the money will be transferred to next. The same principle applies on the other side. The authorities may know how much money is transferred to a certain account, but they cannot track the source. They need to know both the source and the recipient of the money before they could have the slightest clue of what the person is buying. Take one away and they have nothing to work with.

In addition to Tor giving the users anonymity, some cryptocurrencies such as Dash or Zcash also provide their users with cryptocurrency anonymity as one of many security features. In fact, the anonymity provided by those cryptocurrencies could still benefit from Tor. The core Bitcoin project has already integrated Tor's onion routing service to their core network. This integration also provided a greater network protection against target attacks to nodes, of which there are thousands. Since cryptocurrencies are so valuable, they become prime targets for hackers. Therefore, protection is necessary. For those people who mine Bitcoin, anonymity is also very important for their security.

One of the main problems with Bitcoin is how unstable it is. This has been a problem since day one. The price for Bitcoin would skyrocket or plummet rapidly, even on a minute-to-minute basis. With such an unstable value, it is extremely difficult for everyone to use it. Since Bitcoin transactions take time, paying with it seems like rolling the dice. One moment you're paying $1,000 worth of bitcoin, but when the vendor receives the payment, Bitcoin is worth $500. What drives this wild fluctuation?

The governments and the investors contributed to this rapid change in Bitcoin value. Investors now started to crowd into the cryptocurrency industry by putting it on credit cards or taking out equity loans on houses just to be able to buy these e-coins. Regulatory interest from governments across the globe also makes the fluctuations worse. For those who want to make money by making transactions with cryptocurrencies (buy low – sell high) these fluctuations could be very advantageous. However, when the entire Dark Web market depends on Bitcoin for all transactions, everyone needed a more stable currency.

To better understand how damaging this instability is, we need to study the value of Bitcoin and the mechanics of transactions in the Dark Web. The customer purchases Bitcoin and uses it to purchase other products in the Dark Web. The money normally goes into a third-party website (an escrow) before it gets to the vendor for approval. Remember how we talked about this in a previous chapter. Two out of three parties involved (Customer, vendor, site administrator) have to agree before the transaction can go through. Even though the process seems short and simple, this system can still cause financial choke points and delays. The time it takes for the Bitcoin to go from customer to vendor is enough the register vast changes in the price. Should the price plummet, the vendor might make zero dollars profit from their sale.

Illicit markets are not the only ones that are having this problem. Licit markets are also vulnerable to the change in Bitcoin's price. Luckily for the licit markets, they have a solution to stabilize the volatility of Bitcoin's value. According to Jerry Brito, the executive director of Coin Center, a nonprofit research and advocacy organization for cryptocurrencies, merchants could still accept Bitcoins or other forms of cryptocurrencies, even though they want to avoid volatility. A solution could be the use of a service that can automatically convert Bitcoin or other forms of cryptocurrencies into standard currency. That way loses from drastic changes in value can be avoided.

Luckily, such services do not extend to the illegal markets. Therefore, vendors and buyers alike have very few means to cope with the wild fluctuation. In some cases, drug dealers urge their customers to release the money from the escrow even before the product arrives. That is because they fear that they may end up with less money. Some other marketplaces have built their own mechanisms to cope with the change in value. The first Silk Road website also had such a mechanism in place. Still, many other illicit markets do not have access to such a technology. Therefore, many orders are being canceled. The downside is that this also contributes to the volatility of Bitcoin, which hinders the rise of licit markets on the Dark Web. This volatility causes a vicious circle that still hinders progress to this day.

If we are being honest. The only problem with Bitcoin's value fluctuation is when the price plummets. If it goes up, then everyone is quite content. In certain forum posts on the Dark Web, some vendors said that they made more money by just not exchanging their Bitcoin as opposed to selling illegal products. When the price goes down, however, then the vendors are not inclined to sell their goods. According to a cryptocurrency researcher who uses a pseudonym known as Gwern Branwen, upward volatility is largely a good thing for the Dark Web markets since everyone gets more than they bargained for. When the prices crash, the vendors are at a risk of incurring losses from their sales.

Another problem with Bitcoin is the change in the cost of the transaction. All Bitcoin transactions are recorded in a public ledger that is decentralized. So, when someone makes a transaction with Bitcoin, the Bitcoin miners in the network solve cryptographic puzzles to verify and log that transaction. As a reward, the miners are rewarded with a small amount of money in Bitcoin. When there is an increase in the use of Bitcoin, the demand for a transaction also increases. The price of a Bitcoin transaction sometimes spikes as high as $55.

For investors, the price is negligible. For someone who wants to buy cheap products, the cost of transactions could even exceed the price of the product. It really makes no sense to spend $50 in transaction fee when the product only costs $30.

Both aspects, transaction costs, and delays have pushed many participants in the Dark Web markets away from the cryptocurrency. The need for another cryptocurrency raised from that desperation, and there have been many suggestions. Some have suggested using Monero instead since it is a lot more stable. Others suggested taking a riskier route by dealing directly with a dealer. Others believed that it is time that Bitcoin has become obsolete and as one online forum user noted, it takes about 12 to 16 hours to transfer the Bitcoin.

The third problem has to do with anonymity itself. With the increase in Bitcoin popularity, governments are trying to regulate and monitor cryptocurrencies. Even though Bitcoin promised anonymity in transactions, because of how they are publicly recorded thanks to the blockchain system, it is possible to find out a lot about Bitcoin users, and potentially identify the addresses of the Dark Web markets, which makes the micro-laundering or money-laundering process very challenging.

Other cryptocurrencies offer better privacy, and there is a growing tendency to use them instead. Ether and Monero are two of the many alternatives that the Dark Web market users are starting to consider. Although many of them benefited from the surges in price for Bitcoin, its instability put many people off. The people in the Dark Web needed something more stable and efficient. Vendors started asking their customers if they ever considered switching to other forms of cryptocurrencies such as Monero. The idea is to encourage as many people as possible to use them instead of Bitcoin.

Of course, Bitcoin is still relatively common in the Dark Web, but people are slowly moving away from it. Many people believed that Bitcoin allowed their transactions to be quick, efficient, and most importantly, anonymous. At this rate, Bitcoin might fall out of favor soon if it remains unstable. What remains certain is that cryptocurrency will still be used widely in the Dark Web.

Cryptocurrencies are beginning to influence all markets, not only the ones of the Dark Web. Therefore, everything is starting to become more and more connected. The point of this chapter was to highlight how the Dark Web let to the rise, but also the potential downfall of Bitcoin. Still, it is worth mentioning that Bitcoin has led to the birth of a new industry. Right now, there are thousands of new cryptocurrencies out there and more people are getting involved every day. All this arose from the need of a solution in the Dark Web. This shows again, how certain problems from a digital environment have led us to innovation and forced people to think outside the box.

Conclusion

To conclude, the Dark Web may appear to be a thick forest populated by criminals. However, when we observe it in detail, everyone could come to realize that, although illegal business is operating here, the way it is done could be used for legitimate business as well. In fact, the Dark Web may as well be the future of the Internet. A place where everyone is able to browse without the fear of having his or her identity revealed. It offers the freedom that many people want. However, we all should not forget that anything can be used for an ulterior motive. The Dark Web is a prime example. Unfortunately, anonymity itself is a blessing and a curse. A government agent working undercover, an innocent civilian concerned about his privacy, and a terrorist all benefit from online anonymity. It is either everyone or no one, and that is the unfortunate truth. It is up to us to decide what we learn from this, how we are going to move forward in this era and what type of world we want to leave behind.

www.ingramcontent.com/pod-product-compliance
Lightning Source LLC
Chambersburg PA
CBHW070905070326
40690CB00009B/2004